My Adorable
Fox Journal

In this journal there's tons of
space for you to write down all
about you, your life and the fun things
you get up to this year. There are lots of
quizzes and activities, too!

Turn the page to begin...

All about me

Fill in this fun fact file below!

My name: ....

My friends call me: ....

My age: ....

My birthday: ....

I live with: ....

My hair colour: ....

My eye colour: ....

My favourite colour: ....

My favourite food: ....

Three words to describe me: ______________________

____

Draw or stick in a picture of yourself here:

Last year

Write down all the best bits about the past year so you don't forget them!

The things I most enjoyed doing were...

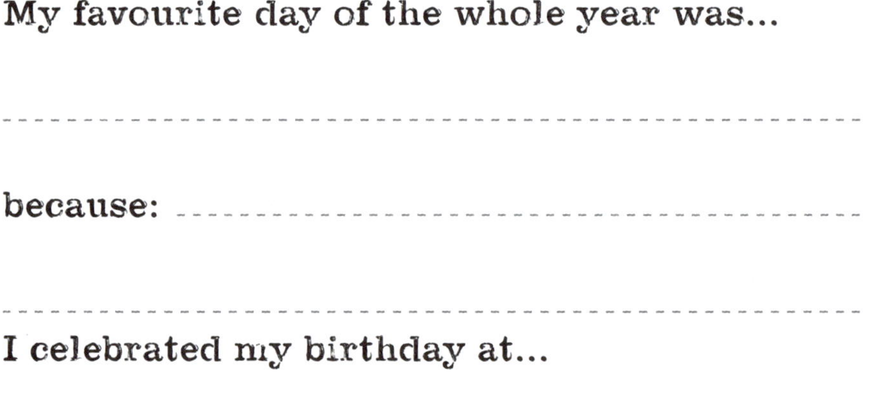

My favourite day of the whole year was...

----

because: -----------------------------

I celebrated my birthday at...

The best present I got for my birthday was...

My best friends were...

The person I'm glad I became better friends with was...

The most exciting place I went to was...

It was so much fun because...

The school lesson I liked most was...

January: Resolution time!

What new things would you like to do this year? Maybe you'd like to join a new club, make a new friend or read some more books. Use this space to write about what you'd like to achieve, then review this page at the end of the year to see how many things you've accomplished. You can do it!

Friends' resolutions!

Ask your friends what their New Year's resolutions
are, then fill in their answers below!

Name:
Resolution:
Name:
Resolution:
Name:
Resolution:
Name:
Resolution:

January
Write about what happened to you this month:

Week 1

Week 2

Week 3

Week 4

February: Celebrity crushes!

Which celebs do you love thinking about?
Valentine's Day is in February, so use these pages to
write down all about your favourite superstars.

My ultimate celebrity crush is...

- -

I love my crush because...

- -

Draw or stick in a picture of your crush here:

My crush's hair colour is...

My crush's eyes are...

I think my crush looks super cute wearing...

Three words I would use to describe them are...

My favourite thing about them is...

Something we have in common is...

If I sent them a Valentine's card, I would write...

This Valentine's Day I would like to...

Dream day out!

If you met your celebrity crush, where would you go? Choose from the ideas below to help you plan an amazing day, then write all about it. Or, if you've got an idea already, skip to page 18 to get started.

I would wear:

jeans and a checked shirt

a pretty dress

a band T-shirt

a skirt with a sparkly top

We would go to:

the park

a bowling alley

the cinema

the beach

a burger bar

a fancy restaurant

We would talk about:

music we both like

our great family and friends

the books we've just read

our favourite weekend activities

The best moment would be:

discovering we like loads of the same things

eating delicious food

being impressed by my crush's outfit

saying we'll stay in touch

Write your story here using the things you have chosen.

Story title: --

By: --

About me and: --

____

Psst! If your story is too long to fit, continue on another piece
of paper, then glue it into your journal afterwards.

February
Write about what happened to you this month:

Week 1

Week 2

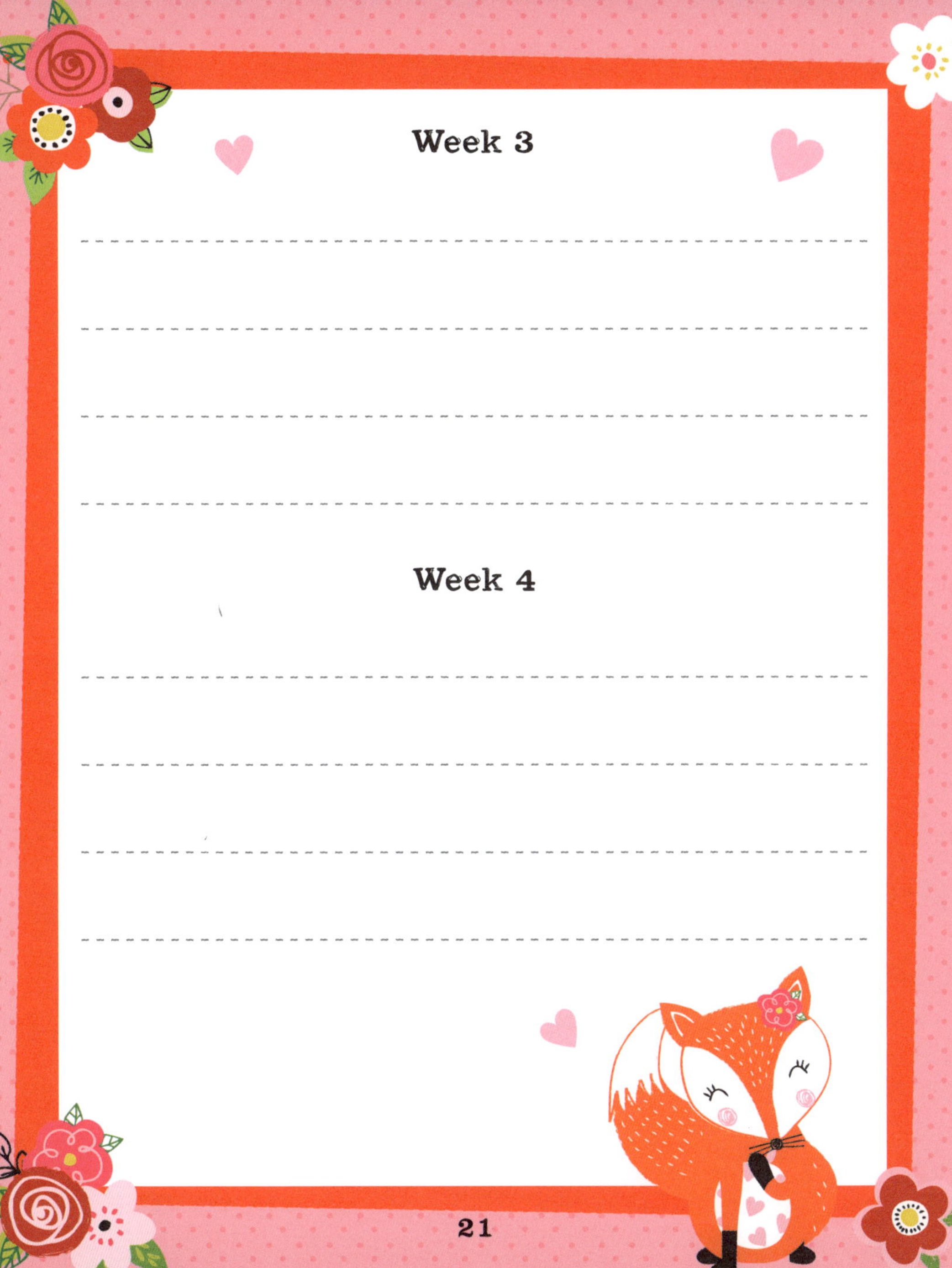

Week 3

Week 4

March: Cute clothes

Do you love clothes and choosing
what to wear? Write down all the essentials
about your clothing collection.

For a casual look, I wear...

When I'm dressing to impress, I wear...

The colour I most like wearing is...

The top item on my clothing wishlist is...

If I could only go to one clothes shop, I'd go to...

My favourite piece of jewellery is...

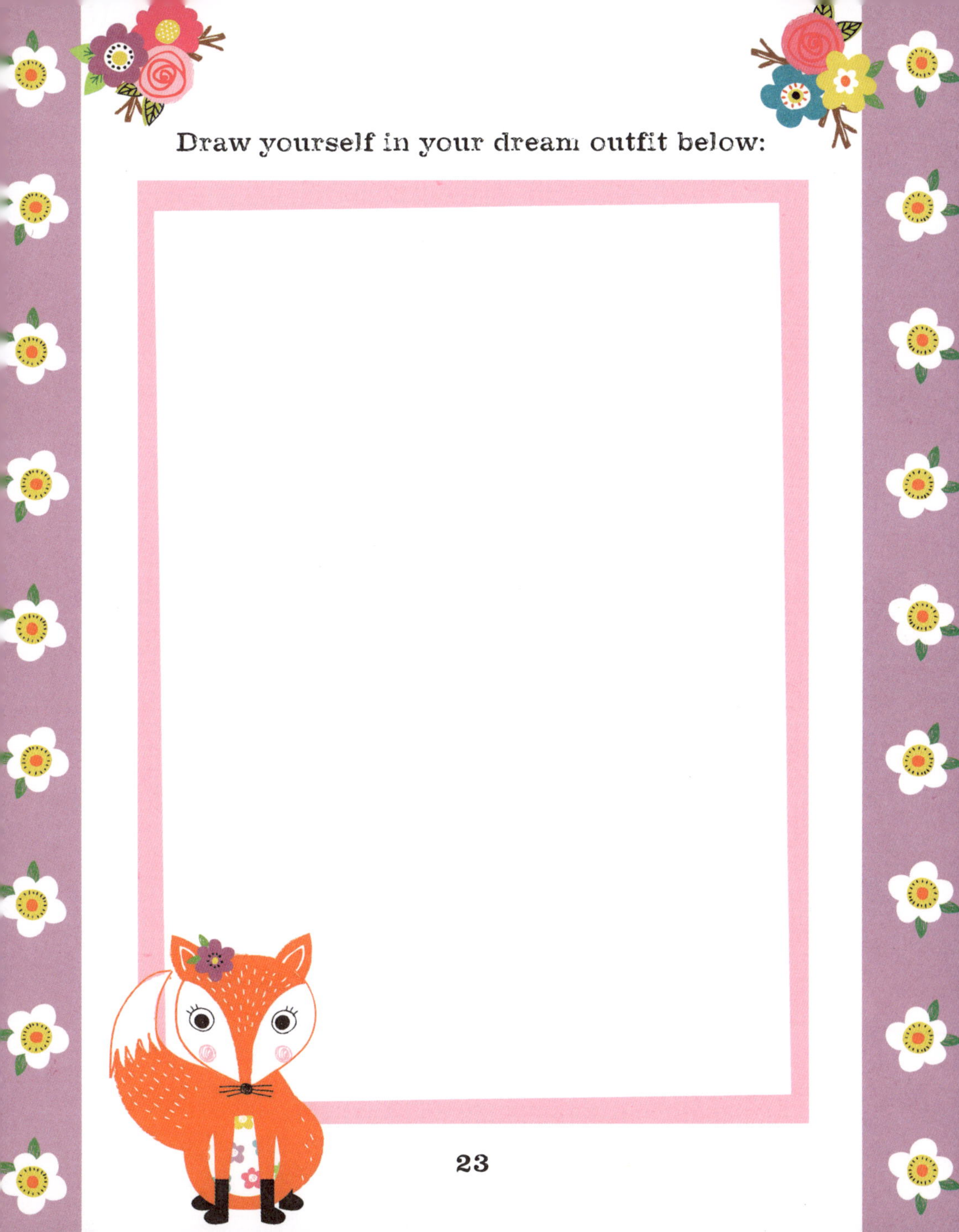
Draw yourself in your dream outfit below:

What's your style?

Do you prefer chilling out in jeans or sparkling in a skirt? Take this quiz to find out what's the best style to make you feel cool and confident.

Your mum buys you a T-shirt as a present. Do you...

Wear it loads – she generally knows what things you like, which is awesome.

Thank her, but say you'd rather choose something yourself next time.

START

Yes

Would you pick wearing trendy trainers over pretty ballet pumps?

No

Characters on your favourite TV show – their clothes are so pretty!

You get your outfit inspiration from...

Magazines – you love studying how models put their looks together.

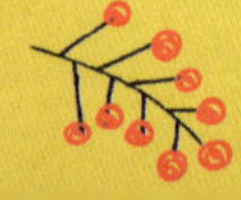

Are all your clothes quite samey?

Y →

Cute and casual

For you comfort is definitely the way to go, and your friends love your laid-back style.

N →

Staying unique

Why follow a trend when you can create your own? You know your own mind – keep on experimenting!

N →

Do you and your friends like wearing matching outfits?

Y →

Pretty perfect

For you, a classic look is always best and your wardrobe is packed with pretty pieces that all your friends want to borrow.

N →

Would you wear a striped top with a polka dot skirt if it was in fashion?

Y →

Fashion fabulous

You're a catwalk queen, and your love of unusual combinations and attention to detail makes you the most stylish person around.

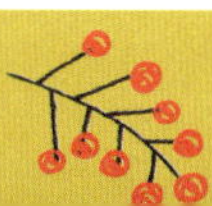

Style confidential!

Could you be a fashion journalist?
Interview two friends about their clothes
and record their answers here.

Friend's name...

Describe your style in three words...

What's your fave item of clothing?

Who are your style icons?

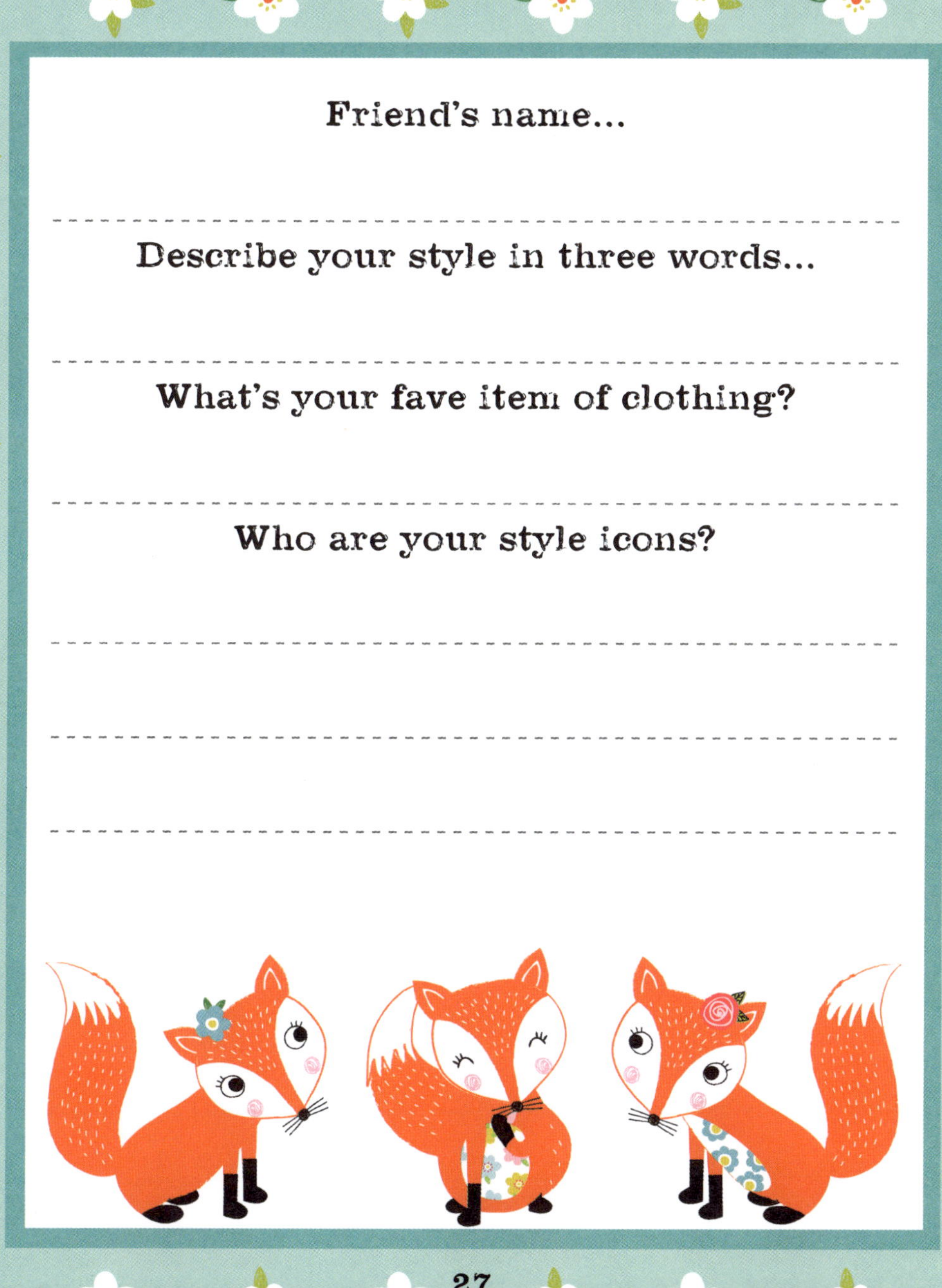

Friend's name...

Describe your style in three words...

What's your fave item of clothing?

Who are your style icons?

March
Write about what happened to you this month:

Week 1

- -

- -

- -

- -

Week 2

- -

- -

- -

- -

Week 3

Week 4

April: Awesome activities

How do you like to spend your time? Maybe
you like reading, hanging out with friends
or doing an exciting sport. Fill in all about
your fun free time here!

My top three hobbies are...

1) --

2) --

3) --

My favourite school club is...

My favourite after-school activity is...

My favourite thing to do on a Saturday is...

The best thing to do on a Sunday is...

The person I most like seeing on
weekends is...

I would spend my dream weekend...

Perfect plans

Not sure what to do this weekend?
Take this quiz to find out what activity
might be fun for you!

1. What do you feel like wearing?

a) Jeans and boots b) A pretty dress

c) Tracksuit bottoms and a baggy top

2. Who do you feel like seeing?

a) Your family   b) Loads of people

c) A few friends

3. What kind of mood are you in?

a) Quiet and reflective   b) Energetic

c) Relaxed

4. What would you like to eat?

a) A homemade meal b) Mini pizzas

c) Chocolate

5. How late do you want to stay up?
a) Not too late – I'm sleepy b) As late as I can
c) Quite late, but not very

6. Do you feel like leaving your house?
a) Maybe   b) Yes, definitely
c) No, I feel like staying in

You chose...

Mostly As – You're in a quiet mood this weekend, so how about chilling at home with your family, catching up on sleep? Sometimes you need a restful weekend after a busy week at school!

Mostly Bs – Clearly a sociable weekend of chatting and making plans is the best option for you. Why not arrange a group activity for all of your friends? How about bowling or going to the park?

Mostly Cs – Dilemma! You'd like to do some something this weekend, but you also feel like relaxing. How about hosting a film night? You can have fun without even leaving the house!

April
Write about what happened to you this month:

Week 1

Week 2

Week 3

Week 4

May: Mood music

Which bands and singers do you
love listening to? Fill in
about your top artists below.

The best current chart song is...

My five fave bands are...

1) --

2) --

3) --

4) --

5) --

My favourite type of music is...

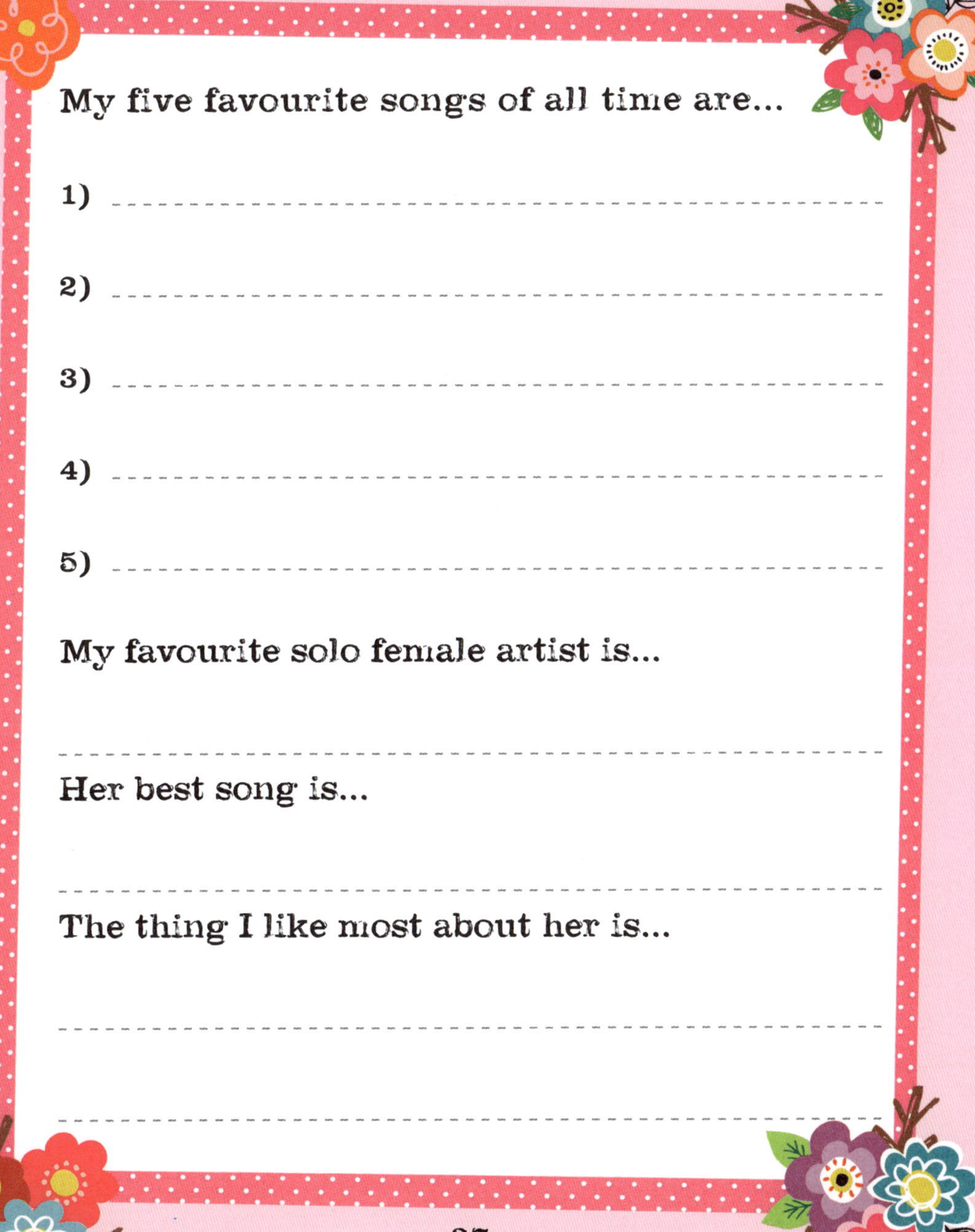

My five favourite songs of all time are...

1) ---

2) ---

3) ---

4) ---

5) ---

My favourite solo female artist is...

Her best song is...

The thing I like most about her is...

My favourite male solo artist is...

- -

His best song is...

- -

The thing I like most about him is...

- -

The artists/band members I think are most good-looking are...

1) -

2) -

3) -

4) -

5) -

The people I'd most like to see live are...

1) --

2) --

3) --

4) --

5) --

The artist I'd most like to be best friends
with is...

The artist with the coolest style is...

My favourite song lyric is...

Songwriting skills!

It's easier than you think to start writing awesome song lyrics. Read below for some tips, then pen your heartfelt words on the page opposite.

1) Write about what you know – your own experiences and feelings will be easiest to express on paper.

2) If beginning is tricky, just try writing one line of an idea and develop it slowly. You don't have to write it all in one go!

3) Say the words out loud to see if they form a good rhythm. Ask a friend or family member to listen as well.

4) Don't panic! Songwriting takes time, so relax and you'll find that inspiration will naturally flow.

Song title:

Lyrics:

May
Write about what happened to you this month:

Week 1

Week 2

Week 3

Week 4

June: Adorable animals!

Foxes aren't the only cute creatures around. Write down all about your other furry favourites below.

My favourite animal is...

- -

Draw or stick in a picture of them here:

Their favourite food is...

They live in...

The most exciting thing about them is...

My best friend's favourite animal is...

If I could see any animal in the world,
I would like to see a...

----

because...

Pick a pet!

Do you dream of owning a cute cat or a mischievious monkey? Take this quiz to find out which perfect pet would suit your personality.

You would rather go on an outing to...

The theatre or cinema – I love watching stories and hearing about other worlds.

Yes

Do you like to break the rules?

A dance or gymnastics show – their dance moves are mega impressive.

No

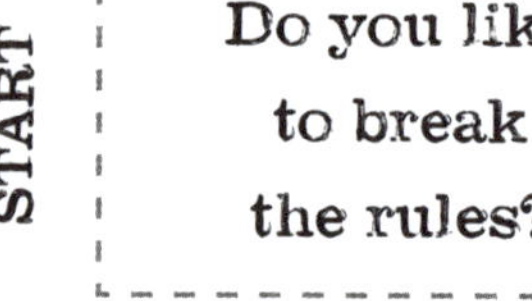

Go for a walk with a friend – the fresh air will be great after being in a classroom.

On the first day of the school holidays, you would like to...

Curl up on the sofa and watch a film – it's so nice to be able to relax after working hard all term.

Do you like wearing bright colours?

Y →

Parrot

With your unique and individual personality, a parrot is the ideal pet for you. You can talk to each other all day long!

N →

Monkey

You are super sociable, and love to be in the spotlight, meaning a monkey to play tricks with would be so much fun.

Would you prefer to have one best friend rather than a large group of friends?

N →

Y →

Dog

You are loyal and outdoorsy. Having a dog means you'll have a walking companion and a friend for life.

Do you like being by yourself sometimes, rather than always hanging out with family and friends?

N →

Y →

Cat

You like a bit of time and space now and again to relax, which is completely natural. Having a furry friend to snuggle up with sounds purr-fect for you!

June
Write about what happened to you this month:

Week 1

Week 2

Week 3

Week 4

July: Best friends forever!

Use the space below to record loads of details about your BFF. If you don't know some of the answers, just ask them! Best friends are always learning new things about each other.

My best friend's name is...

Their age is...

Their middle name is...

Their eyes are...

Their hair colour is...

Their star sign is...

Their favourite food is...

Their favourite colour is...

Their favourite film is...

Their favourite book is...

Their dream job would be...

We are best friends because...

Friendship fact files

Who else is in your friendship group? Fill in all about your other amazing friends below.

My friend's name is...

Draw or stick in a picture of them:

We've been friends for...

The thing I like most about them is...

My friend's name is...

Draw or stick in a picture of them:

We've been friends for...

The thing I like most about them is...

My friend's name is...

Draw or stick in a picture of them:

We've been friends for...

The thing I like most about them is...

My friend's name is...

Draw or stick in a picture of them:

We've been friends for...

The thing I like most about them is...

July
Write about what happened to you this month:

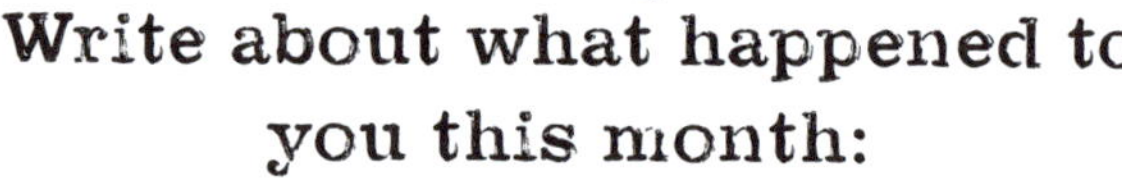

Week 1

Week 2

Week 3

Week 4

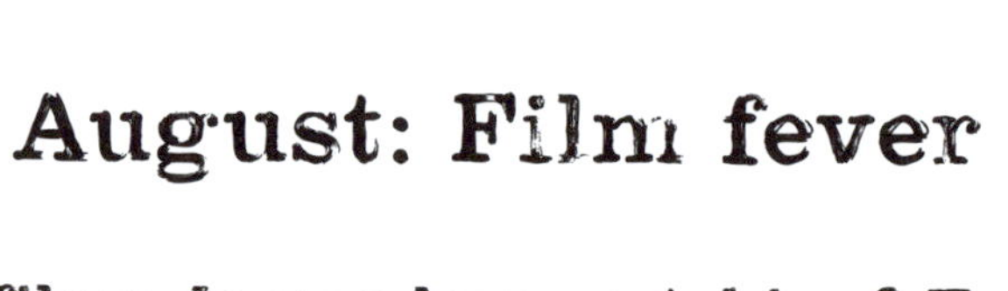

August: Film fever

Which films do you love watching? Everyone has their favourites – write down all of yours!

My top 5 films are...

1) --

2) --

3) --

4) --

5) --

My favourite actress is...

My favourite actor is...

The last film I saw was...

The character I'd most like to be best friends
with from a film is...

---

because...

The actress/actor I'd most like to play me in
a film is...

The first film I remember watching is...

Would you rather?

Think about the options below, then tick the ones you prefer. Consider carefully – it could be tricky to decide! Once you've finished, ask your friends all the questions too!

Would you rather...

watch a film with a happy ending
OR
watch a film that makes you cry?

know the plot beforehand
OR
be completely surprised at the time?

eat sweet popcorn
OR
eat salty poporn?

watch a scary film

OR

watch a funny film?

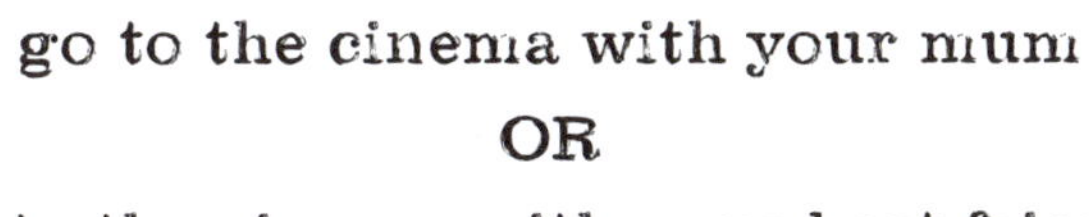

go to the cinema with your mum

OR

go to the cinema with your best friend?

never watch a film again

OR

never listen to music again?

watch a film about friendship

OR

watch a film about romance?

leave the minute the film is over

OR

stay for the end credits?

watch three films in a row

OR

watch five television episodes in a row?

What's your film star name?

Find out your famous film star name!
Simply look at the lists below and combine
the month you were born in (which will be
your first name) with the date you were
born (which will be your surname).

For example, if you were born on the 24th of
April, your name would be Ash Sparkleton!

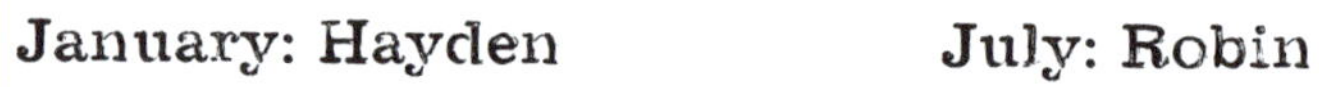

MONTH (first name)

January: Hayden
February: Georgie
March: Harper
April: Ash
May: Indigo
June: Storm

July: Robin
August: Frankie
September: Jessie
October: Charlie
November: Skye
December: Taylor

DATE (surname)

1st : Holmes

2nd: Sparks

3rd: de la Courtney

4th: Aspen

5th: Moonshine

6th: Jazzy

7th: Panther

8th: Royal

9th: Delaney

10th: Sapphire

11th: Salentino

12th: Dazzle

13th: Mangosteen

14th: Noir

15th: Flamingo

16th: Velveteen

17th: Pepper

18th: Heartbreak

19th: Victory

20th: Jingle

21st: Shimmerberry

22nd: Caramel

23rd: Marigold

24th: Sparkleton

25th: Montana

26th: Poison

27th: Glow

28th: Pepino

29th: Topaz

30th: Stardust

31st: Lollipop

My film star name is...

August
Write about what happened to
you this month:

Week 1

Week 2

Week 3

Week 4

September: School time!

Do you look forward to going back to school after a holiday? Fill in all about your school below.

My school is called...

- -

My head teacher is called...

- -

My favourite teacher is called...

- -

My favourite lesson is...

- -

My least favourite lesson is...

- -

My favourite food to have at lunchtime is...

- -

If you could wear anything you wanted to school, what would you choose? Design your dream outfit below. Don't forget to add your ideal school bag and shoes as well!

All grown up!

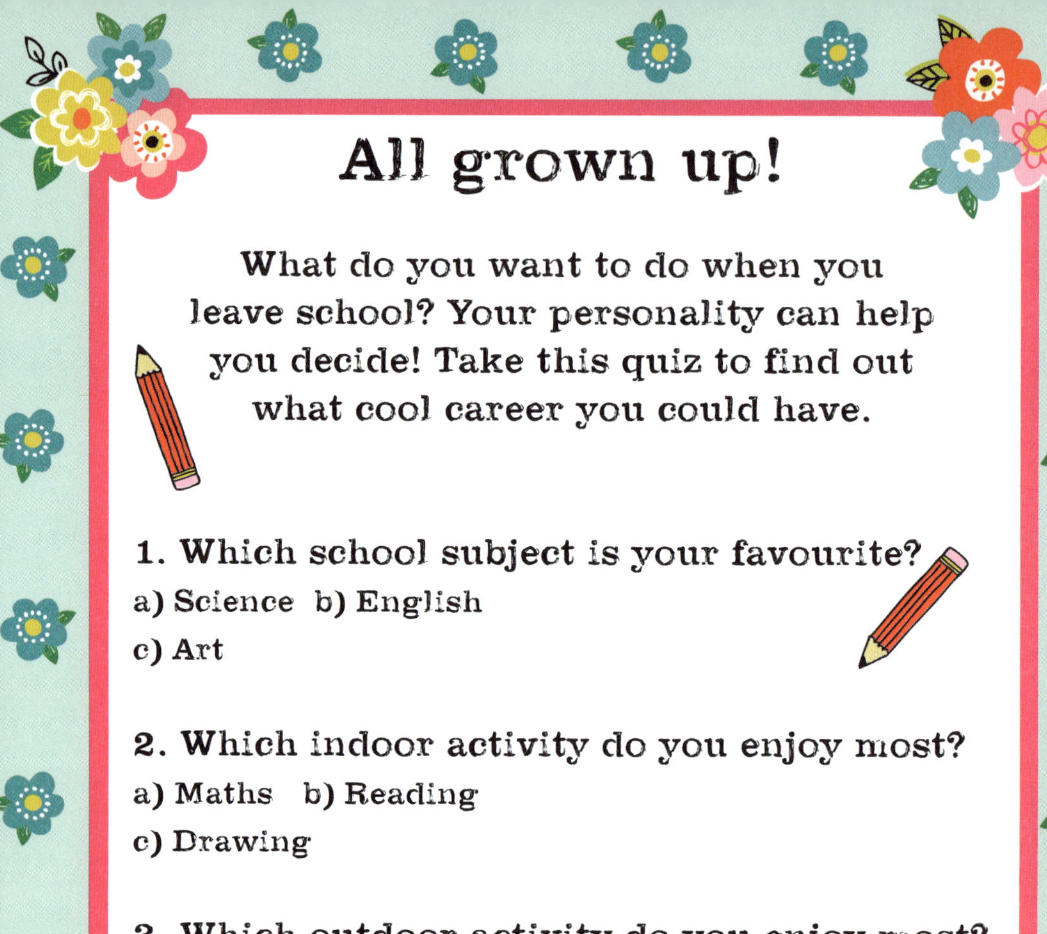

What do you want to do when you leave school? Your personality can help you decide! Take this quiz to find out what cool career you could have.

1. Which school subject is your favourite?
a) Science b) English
c) Art

2. Which indoor activity do you enjoy most?
a) Maths   b) Reading
c) Drawing

3. Which outdoor activity do you enjoy most?
a) Looking for animals   b) Cycling with friends
c) Taking nature photos

4. Which word describes you best?
a) Thoughtful b) Chatty
c) Creative

5. What type of films do you like watching?

a) Documentaries b) Romantic comedies

c) Dramas

6. What colour is your bedroom?

a) Blue b) Black and white

c) Multicoloured

You chose...

Mostly As – You're thoughtful, clever and you love science – being a doctor or a vet would be the ideal job for you. Keep working hard and before you know it you'll be helping real patients!

Mostly Bs – With your love of reading and hearing about other people and their lives, you would make a brilliant journalist. Why not start interviewing people now to practise?

Mostly Cs – Your artistic side is a large part of your personality, so you could make it into a career as well. How about becoming an artist, a designer or a photographer?

September
Write about what happened to
you this month:

Week 1

Week 2

Week 3

Week 4

October: Fun foods!

Who doesn't like interesting
ice cream flavours and yummy cakes?
Write down all about your fave foods.

My favourite meal of the day is...

My favourite food is...

My favourite dessert is...

My favourite chocolate or sweet is...

My favourite fruit is...

If I could only eat one food forever, I would eat...

 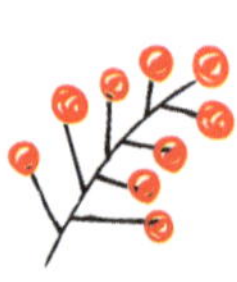    

Create your dream three-course meal below!
What will you have?

MENU

Starter

- -

Main Course

- -

Dessert

- -

Drink

- -

Which delicious dessert are you?

Are you a crumbly cookie or a swirly cupcake? Take the quiz below to find out!

Apple pie

You're sweet and understanding – just like a classic apple pie!

Chocolate-chip cookie

You're fun, easy-going and popular – just like a scrumptious chocolate-chip cookie!

Cheesecake

You love luxury and leading your life with a touch of glamour – just like a fabulous cheesecake!

Cupcake

You're cute and colourful with an artistic side – just like an eye-catching cupcake!

Chocolate-chip cookie recipe!

Wow your friends with these tasty treats. Ask an adult to help you make them – they're super simple!

You will need:

- 225g butter
- 100g caster sugar
- 200g brown sugar
- 1 teaspoon vanilla extract
- 2 eggs
- 350g chocolate chips (or any type of chocolate crumbled up)
- 350g plain flour
- 1 teaspoon bicarbonate of soda
- 1 teaspoon salt

How to make them:

1. Ask an adult to preheat your oven to 190°C/375°F/ gas mark 5.

2. In a large bowl, combine the butter, caster sugar, brown sugar and vanilla extract. Stir until this is

light and fluffy, then beat in the eggs.

3. Weigh out your flour into a medium-sized bowl and combine it with the bicarbonate of soda and salt. Then fold it into your sugar and butter mixture. Finally, add in your chocolate chips (or crumbled chocolate) and stir. You've now made your cookie dough!

4. Start taking small amounts of dough and rolling it into balls. Place the balls on two baking trays with lots of space between them. Bake them for 10–12 minutes, depending on how gooey you like them.

5. Leave them to cool on the baking trays (or on a wire rack), then share with friends. Delicious!

Psst! This recipe makes enough for approximately 12–15 cookies, depending on how big they are.

October

Write about what happened to
you this month:

Week 1

- -

- -

- -

- -

Week 2

- -

- -

- -

- -

Week 3

Week 4

November: Brilliant books

Do you love getting lost in a good story? Books can be interesting, funny and they make you cleverer. Amazing! Fill in all about your fave reads below.

My five favourite books are...

1) --

2) --

3) --

4) --

5) --

My favourite author is...

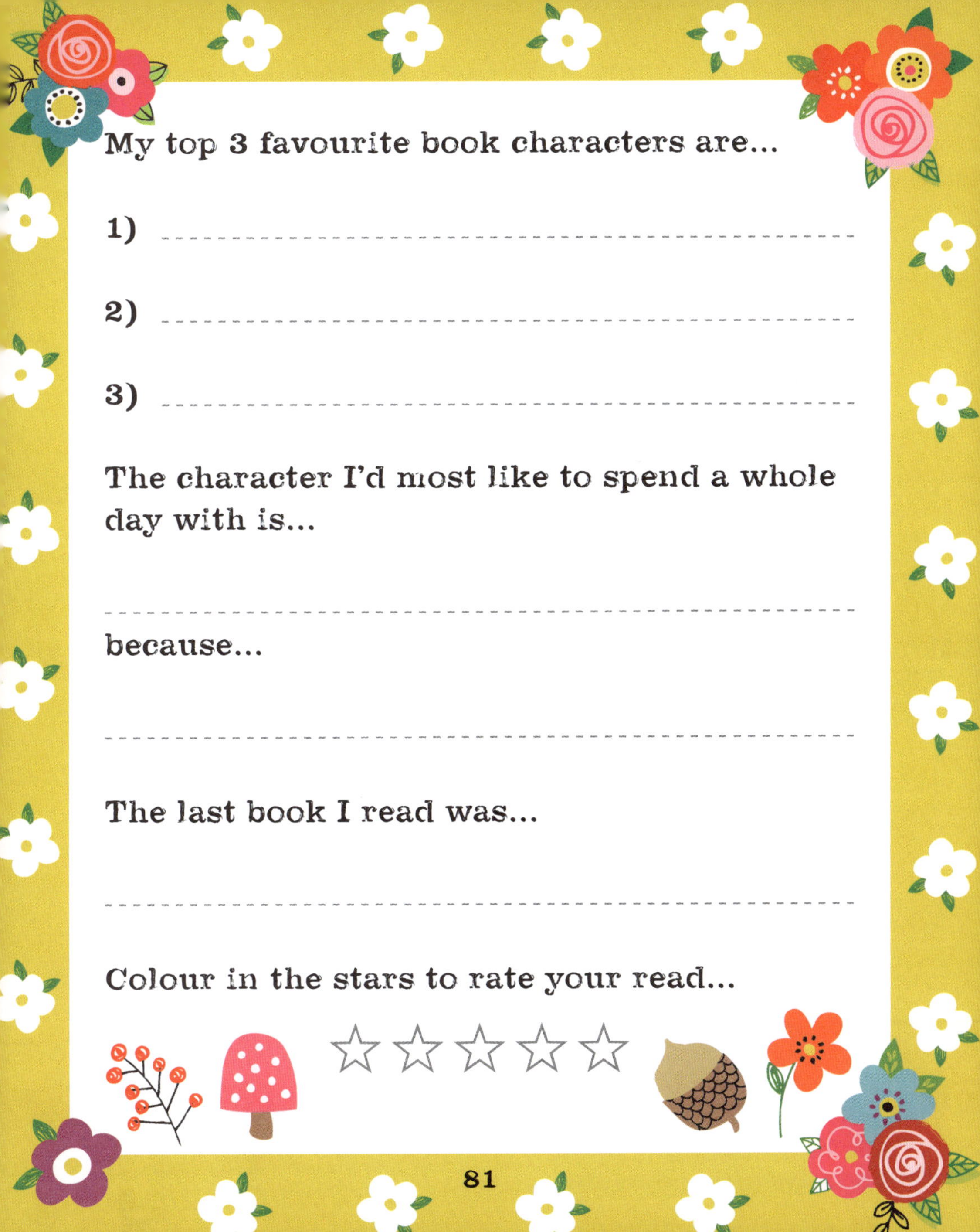

My top 3 favourite book characters are...

1) ....

2) ....

3) ....

The character I'd most like to spend a whole day with is...

because...

The last book I read was...

Colour in the stars to rate your read...

Write it down!

If you were going to write a book, what would it be about? Scribble down the plot below – it can be about anything you like.

Now design the cover for your book. Don't forget to include a title and to add your name as the author!

November

Write about what happened to you this month:

Week 1

Week 2

Week 3

Week 4

85

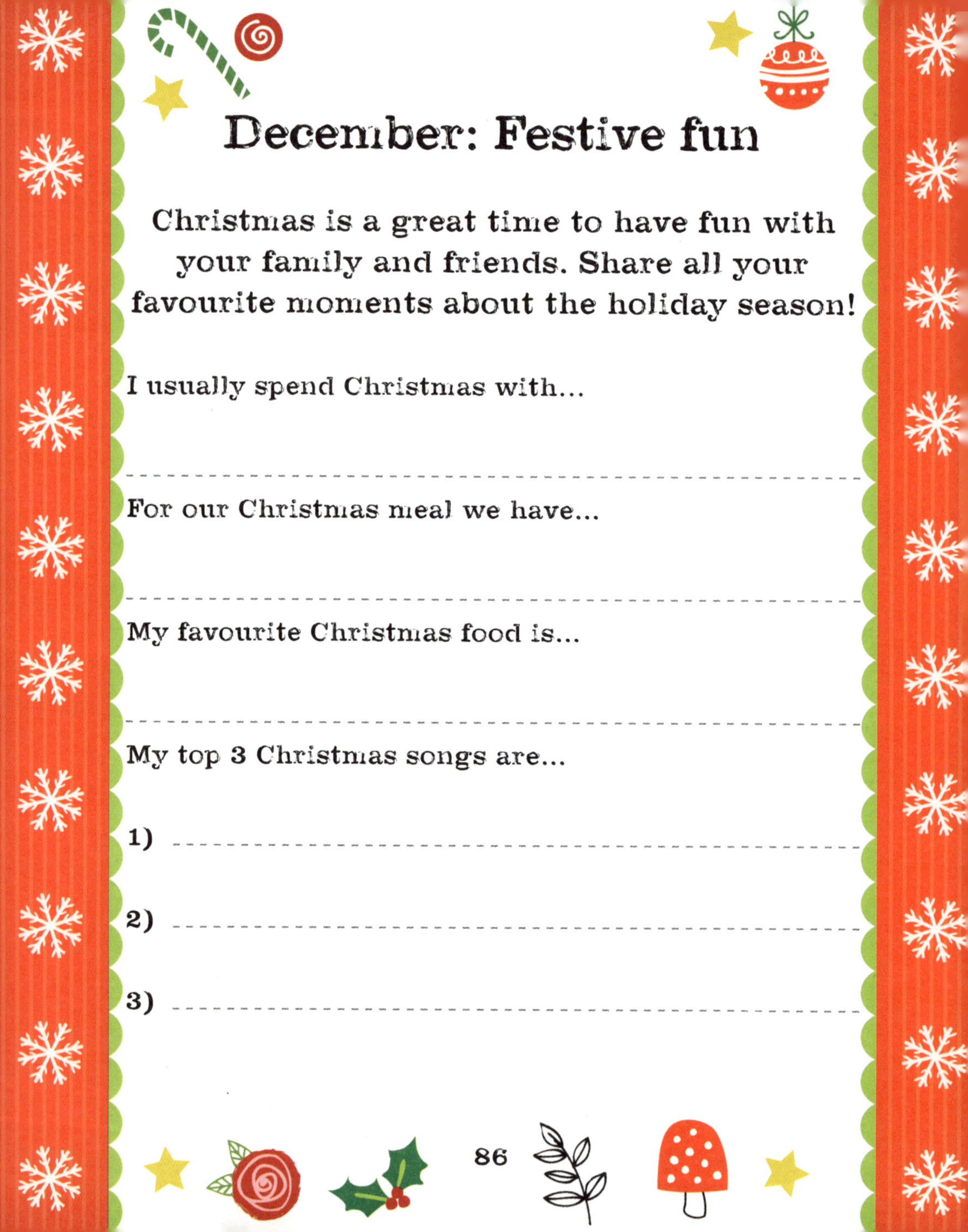

December: Festive fun

Christmas is a great time to have fun with your family and friends. Share all your favourite moments about the holiday season!

I usually spend Christmas with...

For our Christmas meal we have...

My favourite Christmas food is...

My top 3 Christmas songs are...

1)

2)

3)

My favourite Christmas decoration is...

My favourite film to watch at Christmas is...

My favourite game to play at Christmas is...

The best Christmas present I got last year was...

My favourite Christmas memory is...

My favourite part about Christmas is...

because...

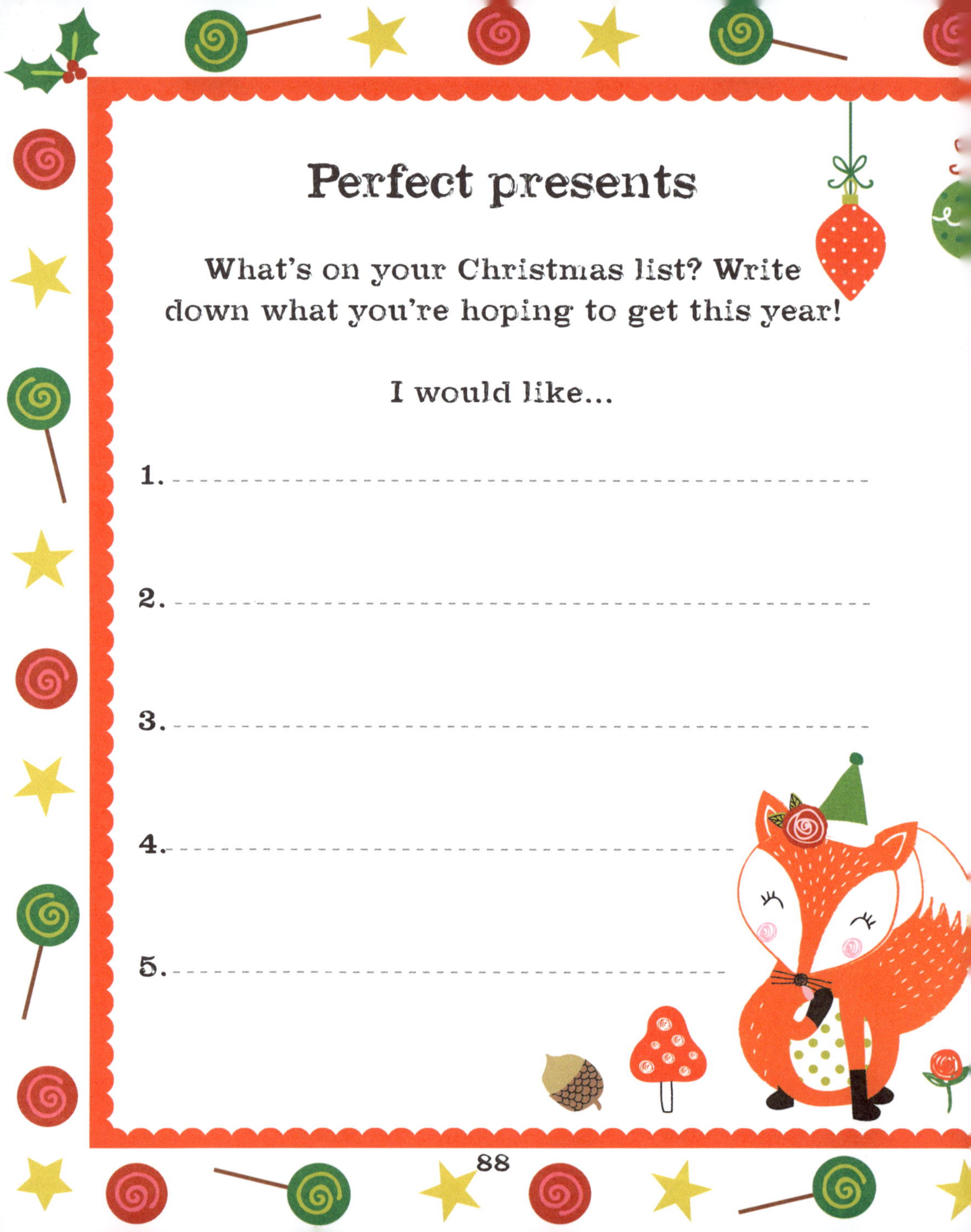

Perfect presents

What's on your Christmas list? Write
down what you're hoping to get this year!

I would like...

1.

2.

3.

4.

5.

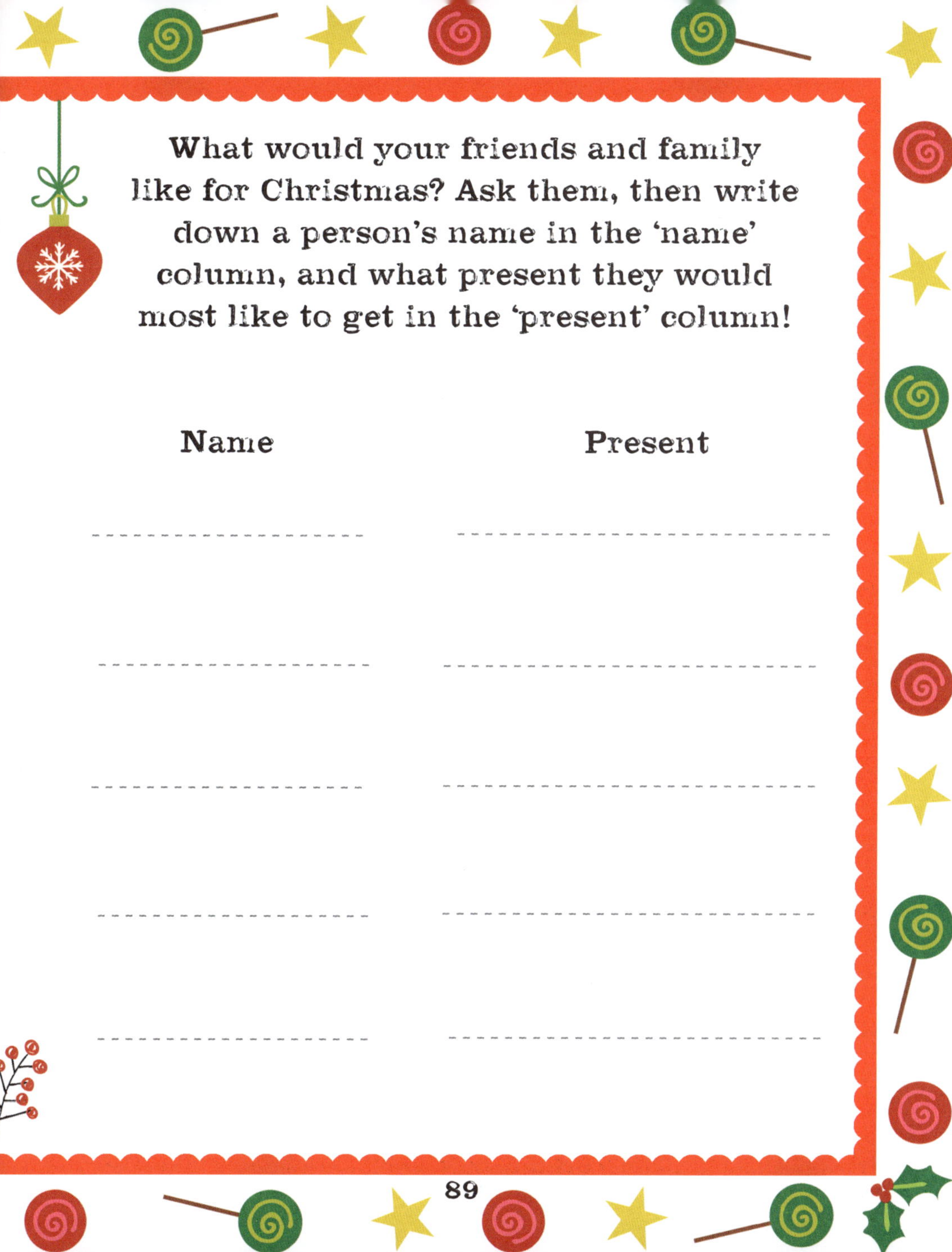

What would your friends and family like for Christmas? Ask them, then write down a person's name in the 'name' column, and what present they would most like to get in the 'present' column!

Name	Present

New Year's Eve!

New Year's Eve is a great way to celebrate the end of the old year and the beginning of the new. What will you be doing this year?

I spent last New Year's Eve with...

My favourite New Year's Eve ever was...

----

because...

My New Year's Eve plans for this year are...

If I could do anything I wanted this New Year's Eve, I would...

Design your ideal New Year's Eve outfit
in the space below. It can be as fancy
or as casual as you like. Don't forget to
include some eye-catching accessories!

December

Write about what happened to
you this month:

 **Week 1** 

 **Week 2** 

Week 3

Week 4

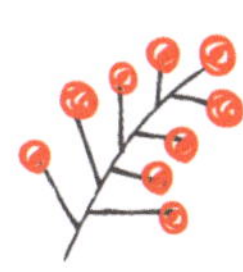

Highlights of the year

Write down all the best moments of your year so you remember them forever.

The most exciting thing I did this year was...

The friend I became closest to this year was...

The most interesting place I went this year was...

The film I most enjoyed watching this year was...

My favourite memory of the whole year was...

because...